# MANDALA
## Relaxation

50 BEAUTIFUL, STRESS-RELIEVING DESIGNS FOR ADULTS

## This book belongs to

_____

_____

ISBN: 9798634040912
© 2020 Pixelated Poppy Press
ALL RIGHTS RESERVED.

Thank you for purchasing this coloring book from
Pixelated Poppy Press!

This book is printed on 55 lb. white paper, with single-sided coloring page designs. Ideal for colored pencils, these designs will also produce beautiful results with various inks and markers.

If you decide to use something other than colored pencils, we recommend that you place a blank sheet or blotter behind the page as you color. Generous spine-side margins make it easy to remove the pages for sharing or for framing your finished work of art.

Test your colors and palette options using the Color Testing Sheet at the back of this book.

Happy coloring!

**BONUS! Look for an offer for FREE
coloring page printables at the
end of this book!**

# COLOR TESTING PAGE

## WE'D APPRECIATE YOUR REVIEW ON AMAZON

Show your support for our small family business and help other colorists discover Pixelated Poppy Press's books!

**To leave your review, find this book on Amazon then scroll to the reviews section and click "Write a customer review."**

We appreciate your purchase and we hope you enjoyed this book.

## THANK YOU SO MUCH!

## GET FREE COLORING PAGE PRINTABLES

Sign up to get FREE printable coloring pages delivered to your email in-box! You'll also be first to hear about new Pixelated Poppy releases and deals on our books.

To sign up, type the URL below into your browser, then follow the instructions.

## http://bit.ly/PPPSIGNUP

Made in the USA
San Bernardino, CA
15 April 2020